MAKING SENSE

~ *of the* ~

EPISCOPAL

CHURCH

MAKING SENSE
of the
EPISCOPAL CHURCH

An Introduction to its History

LEADER'S GUIDE

KEN CLARK, S.T.M., Ed.D. *and* CHARLIE STEEN, Ph.D.

MOREHOUSE PUBLISHING

The authors are grateful for the help given by the Rev. Frank Sugeno, the Rev. Charles J. Cook, and Mr. and Mrs. Harold Booher, Episcopal Theological Seminary of the Southwest, and Mr. Mark Duffy and his staff, Archives of the Episcopal Church, USA, in collecting the documents used in this program. They also appreciate the testing and evaluation of the program provided by the clergy and lay persons of St. Andrew's Episcopal Church, Poughkeepsie, NY; St. John's Episcopal Church, Carlisle, PA; and St. Michael and All Angels Church, Albuquerque, NM.

MOREHOUSE PUBLISHING
PO Box 1321
Harrisburg, PA 17105

Printed in the United States of America
10 9 8 7 6 5 4 3 2

❧ CONTENTS ❧

Introduction

Purpose of This Course

The purpose of this course is to introduce adults to the history of the Episcopal Church from colonial times until the near present.

Audience

This course is designed for adults interested in learning about the history of the Episcopal Church. It can serve as the basis of a Sunday morning or weekday adult class. It can be used in confirmation or catechumen preparation. The course does not presuppose any knowledge of the history of the Episcopal Church, or even of general American and English history.

Methodology

This course is based on primary sources. Excerpts from actual letters, minutes of meetings, histories, and books make up the bulk of the Resource Book. Students read these before class and come ready to engage in activities that foster deeper understandings. This is not a lecture course; however, there is provision for mini-lectures for those who are comfortable with this activity.

Requirements for Leadership

You do not have to be an expert historian to lead this course. The leader is the member of the group who enables the rest of the group to learn. The main requirements are a sensitivity to the needs of others and the ability to keep the group on track.

Theological Orientation

The course is designed to present the classic via media, or middle of the road, understanding of the Episcopal Church. The authors, obviously, have their own prejudices and presuppositions. However, diligent effort has been made to present the broadest possible range of readings in order to present the many-sided aspects of church history. Other than presenting the via media, the authors have no axes to grind and do not intend to engage in any partisan debates through the medium of this course.

Course Structure

There are six Units in the Resource Book, each of which can be covered in one hour. However, an hour and a half to two hours for each session is possible and practical. Special activities for these longer sessions are included. We have intentionally provided more material in each Unit than can ever be covered in class. Be sure to inform your students of this. Their independent work on this material will give them a much fuller understanding of the church than if we had included only enough material for class time. Each session begins with an opportunity for students to note, briefly, things learned in preparation, as well as to ask questions.

Unit Structure

Each Unit of the Resource Book contains primary readings, as well as opportunities for personal reflection and notation. These are for the "students' eyes only," and no one should ever be pressured to share them. Of course, if a student chooses to discuss some of these in class this is quite permissible. Each Unit of the Resource Book concludes with questions designed to review and focus what was learned in the readings. Some of these form the basis for the group activities. Each Unit of the Resource Book begins with Getting Started, a brief historical introduction to set things in context. There is a list of Helpful Words and Concepts at the end of each Unit of the Resource Book, as well as suggestions for further reading. Students should be encouraged to scan the word list before reading the Unit so as to be aware of explanations of unfamiliar terms.

Educational Theory

The most effective learning has four essential parts:
1. Gathering data
2. Responding to the data cognitively
3. Responding to the data affectively
4. Sharing with others

Gathering Data

Most of us are familiar with the lecture method of gathering data. When combined with outside readings this is, of course, an effective way for adults to learn. However, it is not the only way. It is possible for adults to come to class prepared to discuss material they have read beforehand. In this manner, many different interpretations of the data, not just the teacher's, are possible. In this course, provision is made for mini-lectures by the leader or group members. These are not required; however, they are quick and efficient ways to gather data about material not included in the readings. Most of us learn best if a variety of ways of gathering data are included in a course. We have provided several ways to do this in each Unit. Pick the one(s) with which you and the class are most comfortable.

Responding to the Data Cognitively

Responding to data cognitively—thinking about the material—is the way most of us are most familiar with learning. We hear, see, or read something, think about it, and then include it in our minds or discard it. There are many places in the Resource Book for students to make notes as they read in preparation for class sessions. There are also group activities included in each Unit to reinforce cognitive learning.

Responding to the Data Affectively

Responding to the data affectively—with feelings or emotions—can also be described as experiential learning. In whatever ways we want to describe this phenomenon, the fact remains that maximum learning is never achieved if only the cognitive domain is stimulated. We have all known "polly parrots" who could recall masses of data, but could not apply any of it to their own or others' lives. In this course, there are many activities designed to enhance affective learning. Some of these involve simple art projects: be prepared to encounter resistance from some adult learners the first time they try one of these. However, all of the activities have proven to be very helpful to adults. You also need to be sensitive to the fact that group processes have often been designed to manipulate people or to compound group ignorance. The activities in this course have been designed to avoid both of these results. You must, however, be prepared for some initial resistance, especially from students who have had negative experiences with small-group work.

Sharing with Others

Most of us, in our schooling, have shared information by taking tests. Tests have great value in helping us focus our thoughts and in bringing together our cognitive and affective responses to data. But, tests are not the only means to accomplish these important aspects of learning. In each Unit there are activities designed to help students share with others.

It is important to recognize that adults do not learn like children. The rhetorical question, for example, does little other than raise adults' anxiety levels. This is true of most questions from the leader. Not much is gained by making everyone afraid of being embarrassed by being put on the spot.

It is also important to accept the reality that good learning requires commitment. Church courses that do not start and end on time, that do not require the purchase of a book, that do not require preparation, do not accomplish as much as those that require all of these things.

Structure of the Leader's Guide

The Leader's Guide provides an introductory thought for each Unit, including a short statement of purpose of the session. Please read this before you begin preparation. A description of things you will need for the session follows. Next is an opening activity, including a prayer. The central part of the session will be devoted to group activities and/or mini-lectures. Several are suggested for each session. Choose those you think will work best for you. Feel free to modify them for your group. After one or more group activities, there will be time for closure. Do not skip this under any circumstances.

One final note about spelling and punctuation. In the main, we have translated the English of earlier times into modern American to make reading more comfortable. When we have changed any words, they are placed in brackets. We have left some of the traditional English spellings, like "neighbour," intact, because the meaning is clear and we think this helps students stay aware of the English influence on this country. We left some of the punctuation in titles as it appears in the original because, even though different from today's style, it is still clear and easy to read. In the past, dashes were sometimes used as we use commas and periods. In those readings where this was the practice, we have preserved the original.

1 UNIT ONE
Early Colonial Experience

Introductory Thought

Urban T. Holmes III was a perceptive commentator on the Episcopal Church. Think about his words here:

> I have never known two Episcopalians to agree totally, and the fact that we can admit our disagreements is only indicative of our Anglican freedom to acknowledge the polymorphous nature of all human knowing, something not every Christian body is comfortable admitting.
>
> I would argue that my approach is reasonable. I am not saying that it is always analytical or that I have sought to prove my position. This is not what I think Anglicanism intends by being reasonable. By "reasonable" I mean that the argument does not violate in any obvious way a reflective, balanced examination of experience by one who believes himself in love with God.[1]

As you begin this course, commit yourself to enabling the class members to be "reasonable" with each other. This first Unit focuses on the early Colonial period. The readings may cause some concern, because they clearly show that religious freedom in the modern sense was not on the agenda of the founders.

What Is Needed for This Session

A copy of the Resource Book for each student, copies of *The Book of Common Prayer*, newsprint and markers, or a blackboard and chalk, $8\frac{1}{2}$ x 11 construction paper and non-permanent markers (the permanent markers bleed and smell!)

Beginning the Session

Pass out the Resource Books as students arrive. If you need to collect money for these, ask a member of the class to take responsibility for doing so. Ask each person to make a place tag by folding a piece of construction paper lengthwise and printing his or her name on both sides. At the appointed hour, pass out copies of *The Book of Common Prayer*. Begin the session with the Litany of Thanksgiving on pages 578-579. Because this session focuses on the founding of the church in America, this litany is appropriate.

After the litany, tell the class that introductions will come a bit later. Begin by going over each part of the first Unit, simply pointing out the structure of the Unit. Do not take time to read it now. Then, take care of any housekeeping activities. Do not let this take more than 5 minutes.

First Activity

Because the students have not had an opportunity to read their books prior to class, the first session includes reading parts of the first Unit. The first eight readings are used for this activity. Assign one to each member of the class. If there are more than eight members, assign more than one person the same reading. If there are less than eight, summarize the extra readings yourself. Have students read their assignments and prepare one sentence summaries. Allow 5 minutes, then call time and ask each person to introduce him or herself and give a summary of the assigned passage.

After all have made their introductions and summaries, use the "I learned" technique. This is a simple activity in which those who wish to respond do so by beginning with " I learned. . ." and completing the sentence. If you wish, you can follow with an "I was surprised by. . ." activity. Do not force anyone to respond in either of these activities.

Second Activity

Divide the participants into three small groups. Assign the following from the Resource Book:

Group 1 — Reading Nine

Group 2 — Readings 10 and 11

Group 3 — Reading 12

Ask each group to choose a reporter and to prepare a short (3 to 5 minutes) report which answers these questions: First, what were the relationships between the Church of England people and the Puritans in New England? Second, can you think of any contemporary situations that are similar to these?

Allow 10 minutes for preparation. Gather the groups and ask for the reports.

If You Have an Hour and a Half—Add This Activity

Reassemble the three small groups. In this activity three forms of church polity are to be studied. Assign one group the episcopal; the second, presbyterian; and the third, congregational. Tell the students that short definitions of each of these are found in the Helpful Words and Concepts section at the end of the Unit. Ask each group to begin by reading the definition of their assigned form of polity. After doing the reading, each group's task is to list examples of its form of church polity that are present in the modern Episcopal church. For example, the annual parish meeting may be understood as an example of congregationalism in the Episcopal church. Allow 15 minutes for preparation and 10 minutes for presentation.

If You Have Two Hours—Add This Activity

With the whole group, discuss as many of the questions in "Pulling Everything Together" as possible.

Closing Activity

Allow 5 minutes for a closing activity. Begin by emphasizing that the remaining five Units will assume that everyone has read the readings before class. Also, group members must bring their Resource Books to each session. Encourage the students to read those in this Unit that they did not read in this session. If you want group members to give the mini-lectures suggested in Unit 2 of this guide, ask for volunteers to meet with you after class for the full assignment. Ask everyone to meditate silently for one minute about the work done in the session. After a minute, ask the students to think of one word which sums up their experience in this session. Ask for volunteers to tell their word. In the last minute, close with the prayer for missions found at the top of page 58 of *The Book of Common Prayer*.

Special Note: We cannot overemphasize the importance of beginning and ending on time. In the succeeding classes you may find that the best discussion begins when there is only 5 minutes left in the session. Do not be tempted to extend the session. Do not even consider asking the group if this is all right because there is no really acceptable way to say it isn't. The result of going overtime may be growing absenteeism. If what is tempting you to extend the session is really important or interesting, it will be just as important or interesting later, perhaps at the next session.

2 UNIT TWO
Later Colonial Years

Introductory Thought

John F. Woolverton comments on the uniformity, comprehensiveness, and diversity of the Episcopal Church when he says the following:

> . . .The Episcopal Church contributed important elements to the national religious equation. Her Puritanism in Virginia in the seventeenth century produced new and permanent institutional configurations with respect to the role of the laity in religious affairs. In the eighteenth century, the moderate Enlightenment was brought to bear on the intellectual scene through her theologians, both English and American, with far-reaching and long-lasting results. Ironically, she contributed as well to the revival of Puritan evangelicalism in the Great Awakening in ways which proved anathema to many of her members. For those who increasingly came to yearn for a civilization with more culture and tradition than America afforded at the time, the colonial Church of England provided closer ties with English culture, customs and even language. In the conduct of Christian worship her liturgical formularies provided a certain stateliness for those who required such a quality. In addition she furnished worshipers with that kind of churchly comfort which assured them that they were part of a long, unhasting tradition, even if in fact it had only begun with the Elizabethan settlement of 1558. That numerous Americans came to uphold the values inherent in king, country, national religion, and empire as the eighteenth century progressed was in part the church's doing.
>
> And, as if these elements were not enough to make her history a matter of moment, there was the principle of uniformity. This principle was in retrospect the special "burden"—

even curse?—which the colonial Church of England bore in relation to the rest of the country's churches. So acute were the tensions thus created by her establishments, as well as by those in New England of the Congregational churches, that religious uniformity was to find its settled form not in the triumph of one denomination over another but in the condign resolution of civil religion. In that dawning religious light—or was it a waning one?—all denominational distinctions paled, and towards this end the Episcopal church contributed both negatively and positively: negatively, because when her leaders tried to load the statute books for her benefits and at the expense of others, the impotence of her authority became apparent; positively, because in her own lack of theological definitude, in her confusion, in her comprehensiveness, she declared that the means of grace were many. She thereby anticipated the most basic belief in the religion of the nation.[2]

In this Unit, try to help your students focus on these themes of uniformity, comprehensiveness, and diversity which continue to show that the via media really is part and parcel of the Anglican experience.

What Is Needed for This Session

A copy of the Resource Book for each student who was not present at the first session, copies of *The Book of Common Prayer*, newsprint and non-permanent markers.

Beginning the Session

At the appointed hour, briefly welcome any newcomers and have them make place tags. Pass out copies of *The Book of Common Prayer*. Begin the session with the Litany for Ordinations on pages 548-551 which is appropriate because so much of this Unit focuses on the role of clergy in the colonial church.

After the litany, ask if there are any questions that came up in the readings. Limit this activity to 5 minutes, and simply list the questions on newsprint or a blackboard. If some will be dealt with in the activities, say so now. Short factual questions need not be listed but can be answered by the leader or others in the class.

First Activity

Once again, use the "I learned" technique. Allow no more than 5 minutes and simply ask for volunteers to tell one thing they learned in preparing for this Unit. Try to avoid comments on these, and do not let any debate occur.

Second Activity

Divide the participants into three groups. Give each group a sheet of newsprint and several markers. Ask each group to spend 5 minutes describing how the church was established in the colonies; then, to spend 5 minutes discussing how the church is established today in America. If this causes difficulties, help the groups by suggesting that tax exempt status is a form of establishment. Next, ask each group to prepare a cartoon presentation of the established church in colonial times and today. Ask the groups to limit their drawing time to 5 minutes. There may be some resistance to this activity at first, but groups of adults really do learn to enjoy such activities. After all have prepared the drawings, hang them on the wall and ask each group to present its work with some comments. Allow no more than 5 minutes for reporting.

OR

Present a 10 minute mini-lecture (given either by you, as leader, or by a designated person) on the established church in colonial America. Allow 10 minutes for questions and full group discussion.

If You Have an Hour and a Half—Add This Activity

Reassemble participants in three small groups. In this activity the issue of a bishop for the colonies is be discussed. Ask each group to prepare a list of the arguments for and against a residential colonial bishop. Then ask the groups to prepare one sentence to answer this question: What is the single most important thing that happened to the church in colonial America because there was never a resident bishop? Ask each group to write its answer on one sheet of newsprint and hang it on the wall. After 15 minutes, reconvene and ask each group to report on its list of arguments and comment on its sentence. Be sure to ask whether there are any minority opinions that are not represented in the official report of each group.

OR

Present a mini-lecture (given either by you, as leader, or a designated person) on the consequences of not having a bishop in Colonial America.

If You Have Two Hours—Add This Activity

With the whole group, discuss Benjamin Franklin's abridgement of *The Book of Common Prayer* (Reading 20). If the group is being honest and open, it might be worthwhile to take a vote on how many would like to try his abridgement in a service!

Closing Activity

Allow 5 minutes for a closing activity. If you will use mini-lectures in the next session, ask for volunteers. Then note that Unit 3 will be covered in the next session. Ask everyone to meditate silently for one minute about the work done in this session. After a minute, ask the students to think of the concept that seems to be most important in this Unit. Ask for volunteers to tell what their concept is. In the last minute, close with one of the collects for the Mission of the Church, page 206 of *The Book of Common Prayer*.

3 UNIT THREE
The American Revolution

Introductory Thought

W.W. Manross wrote one of the definitive histories of the Episcopal Church. Some scholars disagree with his assessment that the Episcopal Church wanted to be a neutral bystander in the Revolution. Today, in these times of ecumenical sensitivity, many would not want to call any one denomination or communion "The Church" as Manross does. In addition, the second half of his paragraph quoted here does not really follow from the first half. Be that as it may, his description of the state of the Episcopal Church after the Revolution is succinct and you may want to share it with your students.

Revolutions, like street fights, are likely to be as dangerous to the innocent bystanders as to the participants, and the position of the Church in the American Revolution was, in some sense, that of an innocent bystander. This is not to say that her members did not take sides, for many of them did, but they did not all take the same side, and it is probable that influences other than their Churchmanship governed their decision for or against the rebellion. In spite of the efforts of the opponents (and some of the advocates) of episcopacy to connect that topic with the general controversy, the real issues of the struggle were not ecclesiastical, and the Church had no direct concern in them. Most of her ministers would probably have preferred to remain neutral if they could, though clearly this was an impossibility. Nevertheless, the Church was profoundly affected by the Revolution. When it was over she was compelled to reorganize herself from the bottom up, to obtain from a foreign power the episcopate so long denied here when her members were still subjects of that power, and to find entirely new methods of supporting her services in most of the places where she held them. She was obliged to do all this, moreover, at a time when she had but a fraction of her former number of ministers, and when she was regarded with suspicion in many sections where most of her members had been hostile to the revolutionary cause.[3]

In this Unit, try to help your students understand the great pressure on the Church of England clergy in America during the Revolution, the quest for bishops, the party strife after the Revolution, and the emergence, through compromise, of what we know today as the Episcopal Church today.

What Is Needed for This Session

Copies of *The Book of Common Prayer*, newsprint, and markers.

Beginning the Session

Because a major part of this Unit is devoted to the obtaining of bishops for America, begin the session with the post-communion prayer found in the service for the Ordination of a Bishop on page 523 in *The Book of Common Prayer*. Take a minute to point out this service to your students and suggest that they read it. Note that the old term *consecration* is replaced by the term *ordination*.

After the prayer, ask if there are any questions that came up in the reading. Limit this activity to 5 minutes. You may want to list the questions on newsprint or a blackboard. If some answers will be covered in the activities, say so now. Short, factual questions can simply be answered by the leader or others in the class and need not be listed.

First Activity

If you have had success with the "I learned" technique, continue to use it. If it has not worked well for you, then give a 5 minute mini-lecture on what you, personally, think is the most important thing(s) you learned in this Unit.

Second Activity

Divide participants into two groups. Ask Group 1 to present a brief skit of a meeting between a senior warden who is a Loyalist and the parish rector who is a Revolutionary. Ask Group 2 to present a similar skit with the roles reversed (the senior warden is a Revolutionary and the rector is a Loyalist). The issue that has caused the meeting is what to do about the Prayerbook prayers for the king. Ask the participants to imagine that the two men are friends who have been together in the church for several years and now find themselves on opposite sides. Ask them to present the arguments for and against, and the reasons for the same as concretely as possible. For example, think about what will happen to attendance and offerings, no matter how the question is decided. Allow 10 minutes for preparation and about 5 minutes for each skit. After the skits, ask for questions and discussion of the issues.

OR

Present a 10 minute mini-lecture (given either by you, as leader, or by a designated person) on the plight of Colonial clergy during the Revolution.

If You Have an Hour and a Half—Add This Activity

Reassemble the two groups. Ask Group 1 to present the case for an episcopal form of church government and Group 2 to do the same for the federal form. Allow 10 minutes for presentation. Reconvene and ask for reports. After the reports, ask the full group for examples they know of in the modern Episcopal Church that reflect both forms of church polity.

OR

Present a 5 minute mini-lecture (given either by you as leader, or by a designated person) on the two forms of polity. Follow this with a group discussion and question time. Then ask for examples of each in the modern Episcopal Church.

If You Have Two Hours—Add This Activity

One of the questions in "Pulling Everything Together" says that Benjamin Franklin had a naive understanding of the church. Ask for the group's opinion of this statement and to give reasons.

Closing Activity

Allow 5 minutes for a closing activity. If you will use mini-lectures, ask for volunteers. Then note that Unit 4 will be done next week. Ask for three or four volunteers to tell what they think was most important in this Unit. In the last minute, close with Prayer II, *The Book of Common Prayer*, page 256.

4

Hobart, Griswold, and Friends and Enemies

Introductory Thought

Professor Prichard has written one of the newest texts on the history of the Episcopal Church. In his introduction to the period 1800-1840 he says the following:

> Episcopalians had reacted to the American Revolution in much the same way that their English ancestors had responded to the Glorious Revolution. Some objected to the Revolution and tried to remain aloof from the new republic, much in the same ways English and Scottish nonjurors had done in 1688. A majority of the laity and perhaps 50 percent of the clergy had, however, followed the example of the English Whigs. They saw the Revolution as an extension of individual rights and attempted to remake their church in a more democratic pattern.
>
> The democratic dream was not an exclusive property of the Episcopal Church. Americans of all religious traditions saw the Revolution as an extension of personal liberties. . . By 1800, however, Americans had begun a gradual retreat from some of the ideals of 1776. The equality of blacks and whites, or of men and women, for example, no longer seemed wise goals for many Americans who feared the more radical notions of equality of the French and Haitian revolutions. American fear of a French invasion at the end of the eighteenth century contributed to a more conservative United States in the nineteenth century.
>
> By 1800, American Christians began to look for change from a different direction. The patriots of 1776 had secured greater personal freedom with the force of arms. The citizens of 1800 looked, in contrast, to education. It was the instrument that would both safeguard existing freedoms and pro-

19

vide the opportunities to take advantage of them. It would, in addition, provide a public morality and an identity to a nation of people who could no longer understand themselves simply as English men and women.

Episcopalians, though struggling to recover from the effects of the Revolution, were active in the attempt to educate and edify the new nation. Led by Bishop William White, the only one of the first four bishops to remain active in the national church after 1800, they worked at colleges and secondary schools, founded theological seminaries, and campaigned for public morality.[4]

In this Unit, your students will meet bishops who begin to take a leadership role in defining public morality and in encouraging the church to take things such as confirmation and spiritual growth seriously. They will also encounter an early attempt to create a national church (*The Muhlenberg Memorial*). This was proposed, in part, to ensure a common public morality. The issue of spiritual regeneration—did it happen at baptism or at some later point in life—was a major theological issue, as was the arrival of documents from the Oxford Movement. The latter was an attempt to recover the Catholic heritage of the English church and evolved into what we know as Anglo-Catholicism today. Mission work spread to the expanding frontier with bishops and other clergy moving westward.

What Is Needed for This Session

Copies of *The Book of Common Prayer*.

Beginning the Session

Now that the church had bishops, confirmation became a possibility. Begin the session by saying, together, the prayer on page 418 of *The Book of Common Prayer*. Suggest that your students read the whole service of Confirmation in the next few days.

After the prayer, ask if there are any questions. You may want to list these on newsprint or a blackboard. If some will be covered in the activities, say so now. Short, factual questions can simply be

answered by the leader or others in the class and need not be listed.

First Activity

If you have had success with the "I learned" technique, continue
to use it. If this has not worked well for you, then give a 5 minute
mini-lecture on what you, personally, think is the most important
thing(s) you learned in this Unit.

Second Activity

Divide participants into two groups. Ask Group 1 to report on the
duties and responsibilities of laity as given by Bishop Claggett
(Reading 1). Ask Group 2 to do the same regarding clergy, based
on Bishop Claggett's comments (Reading 1) and Bishop White's
address (Reading 3). Allow 10 minutes for preparation and 5 minutes for each report.

OR

Present a 10 minute mini-lecture (given either by you, as leader, or
by a designated person) covering the responsibilities of clergy and
lay persons as given by Bishops Claggett and White. Follow this
with discussion and clarification for no more than 10 minutes.

If You Have an Hour and a Half—Add This Activity

Reassemble the two groups. Ask Group 1 to summarize the ministry of Bishop Hobart. Ask Group 2 to do the same with Bishop
Griswold. Allow 10 minutes for preparation and 5 minutes each
for the reports.

OR

Present a 10 minute mini-lecture (given either by you, as leader, or
by a designated person) on the ministries of Bishops Hobart and
Griswold. Be sure to emphasize their differences, especially
between the high church and evangelical ideas.

If You Have Two Hours—Add This Activity

Lead a roundtable discussion of *The Muhlenberg Memorial*. Try to relate this to current situations, especially in terms of church union. See whether your students can list reasons that the Episcopal Church did not act on this memorial in any significant way. You may also wish to discuss this in terms of Muhlenberg's commitment to Evangelical Catholicism.

Closing Activity

Allow 5 minutes for a closing activity. If you will use mini-lectures for the next session, ask for volunteers. Then note that Unit 5 will be covered in the next session. Ask for three or four volunteers to tell what they think was most important in this Unit.

In the last minute, close with Prayer 18, *The Book of Common Prayer*, page 820. This is a prayer for the country and is appropriate because of the intense nationalism of the period being studied.

5 UNIT FIVE
The Civil War and Afterwards

Introductory Thought

Professor Prichard cites a Romantic reaction in the nineteenth century. Here are some of his thoughts:

> Episcopalians in the first third of the nineteenth century had made great progress in putting the chaos and confusion of the Revolutionary War years behind them. They had found a new, more aggressive model for the episcopate, had adopted both the Thirty-nine Articles and a uniform Course of Ecclesiastical Studies, and had begun to send bishops to the West. Unlike the generation that had preceded them, Episcopalians maturing after 1800 knew where their church stood on a variety of issues and could be quite explicit about that stance.
>
> This increasingly confident orthodoxy served Episcopalians well in the first third of the century. By 1840, however, America was changing, and many Americans found that the rational approach to theology and the church no longer met their needs. The enlarged textile factories in Lowell, Massachusetts (1813), the newly opened Erie Canal (1825), and the Baltimore and Ohio Railroad (1828) all heralded a more sophisticated, industrialized nation. The triumph of an industrial North over an agricultural South made it all the more clear. Americans were no longer citizens of a frontier agricultural nation. The values of the new industrialized nation were different, and many Americans looked to Christianity to preserve the virtues—a close connection with nature, the intimacy of the frontier family, a sense of awe in creation, and a more spontaneous and expressive way of life—that they attributed to their past. Once Americans

began this search for such a past, they were not content, however, simply to examine their own recent history. Many looked beyond it to Greece and Rome.

Greek Christians, subjects of the Muslim Ottoman Empire since the mid-fifteenth century, had rebelled and gained their independence from Turkey in 1829. The victory caught the imaginations of Americans. They followed the exploits in Greece of British poet George Gordon Byron (1788-1824). They read the "Ode on a Grecian Urn" by John Keats (1795-1821) and built homes in Greek revival style. American college students formed Greek letter fraternities. It was this excitement over things Greek that had led the Episcopal Church to send its first official missionary team to Greece in 1830. . . This attraction of a Greek and Roman past and the nostalgia produced by the industrialization of America challenged the rational orthodoxy of the earlier part of the century. Many Americans at midcentury no longer looked to their churches for a clear exposition of doctrine. Rather they looked to them for mystery, beauty, and a sense of permanence. Episcopalians were as successful as any Protestant church in coming to terms with the new American mood, yet even for them the transition was a difficult one.[5]

This session focuses on the Civil War, controversy over ritual, and the beginnings of ecumenical thought. Some Episcopalians have tried to minimize the extent of the split in the church, north and south, by citing the fact that after the conflict the Episcopal Church, unlike the Methodist and Presbyterian Churches, was quickly re-united. This, of course, is true. However, the readings will show just how deep the divisions were. The controversy over ritual will probably be of most interest to your students. The severity of this issue, had it been understood better in the 1970s, might have put the debates over the revised Prayer Book of 1979 on different ground. One thing that may not come out in the readings is the obvious fact that if a church can invest great time in debating ritual, it must be fairly secure. A church that is about to die or is under secular attack does not have time to devote to arguments over ritual. The latter part of the nineteenth century was a time of great church security, especially for Episcopalians. Episcopalians, from at least the time of William White, and perhaps before, have taken leadership roles in ecumenical discussions. In a new suburb in the authors' hometown there is a hill with four small churches on it—each representing a different brand of Christianity. Many, probably most, in the nineteenth century, just as today, saw nothing wrong in this phenomenon. However, there were voices that questioned the divisions in a church in which the founder had prayed that his followers might all be one. It was out of this reality that Episcopal lay persons and clergy engaged other Christians in attempts to make good on that prayer.

What Is Needed for This Session

Copies of *The Book of Common Prayer*, pens and paper.

Beginning the Session

Because this session spends a considerable amount of time on the nation, begin with Thanksgivings for National Life, *The Book of Common Prayer*, No. 5., pages 838-839. After the prayer, ask whether there are any questions. You may want to list these on newsprint or a blackboard. If some will be covered in the activities, say so now. Short, factual questions can simply be answered by the leader or others in the class and need not be listed.

First Activity

If you have had success with the "I learned" technique, continue to use it. If this has not worked well for you, then give a 5 minute mini-lecture on what you, personally, think is the most important thing(s) you learned in this lesson.

Second Activity

Present a 10 minute mini-lecture (given either by you, as leader, or by a designated person) on how the Episcopal Church in the North and in the South understood what was happening in the Civil War. Follow this with a full group discussion and clarification for not more than 10 minutes.

Third Activity

Divide participants into two groups. Group 1 will be those who supported the new ritual practices in the Episcopal Church. Group 2 will be those who were against. Allow 10 minutes for preparation, then have each group present its arguments, either for or against.

OR

Divide participants into the same two groups with the same attitudes. However, in this activity each group is to prepare a short written "altar guild manual" with instructions on how to conduct the service of Holy Communion. Directions to the priest should be included as well. After 10 minutes, gather as a full group and present the results. Allow 5 minutes for discussion.

If You Have an Hour and a Half—Add This Activity

Present a mini-lecture (given either by you, as leader, or by a designated person) on the Episcopal Church's role in ecumenism in the 19th century. Limit this to 5 minutes with a group discussion following of 15 minutes.

OR

Read aloud the Chicago-Lambeth Quadrilateral in *The Book of Common Prayer*, pages 876-877. You may ask several readers to take turns reading sections. Then spend 15 minutes in a full group discussion of this document. Consider how, if at all, it has been acted on in the years that have transpired since its adoption.

OR

Dr. Huntington makes a very pragmatic comment on ecumenism (Reading 12 in the Resource Book). Read this aloud and spend 20 minutes discussing the issues he raises.

If You Have Two Hours—Add This Activity

Go to the questions in "Pulling Everything Together" in the Resource Book. Discuss as many of these as possible with the full group.

Closing Activity

Allow 5 minutes for a closing activity. If you will use mini-lectures in the next session, ask for volunteers. Then note that Lesson 6 will be done next in the next session. Ask for three or four volunteers to tell what they think was most important in this lesson.

In the last minute, close with Prayer 14, For the Unity of the Church, in *The Book of Common Prayer*, page 818.

6

UNIT SIX

To 1964

Introductory Thought

Once again we turn to Professor Prichard to focus our thoughts in preparation for leading this session. This time we use his *Readings From the History of the Episcopal Church*. We trust that our frequent use of his writings indicates that both of his books should be readily available to the leader of this course. Here is his summary of key events in the period of time under consideration in this session:

> ...the Episcopal Church did make considerable strides during these years toward becoming a more compassionate and inclusive church. Among the accomplishments to which Episcopalians could look as evidence of this change were: (1) At the General Conventions of 1886 and 1892, the Episcopal Church became the first American denomination to go on record as favoring improved conditions for the industrial workers. (2) The 1916 Christian Nurture series, the church's first graded Sunday school curriculum emphasized missions and social action. (3) In 1918 Henry B. Delaney (1858-1928) of North Carolina and Edward T. Demby (1869-1957) of Arkansas became the first black Episcopal (suffragan) bishops to serve in the continental United States. (4) The General Convention of 1919 amended the church's constitution to make the presiding bishop an elective rather than a seniority position. At approximately the same time many individual congregations abandoned perpetual vestries in favor of a rotating leadership, and a "Nation-Wide Campaign" (a coordinated national canvass in 1919) helped individual pledging replace the vestiges of the pew rent system. (5) Professor Vida Scudder (1861-1954) and other Episcopalians interested in more humane national policies supported the Christian Socialist

Fellowship that drew nearly one million votes in 1912. Economist Richard T. Ely (1854-1943) challenged prevailing economic theories that appealed to natural law to give businesses a free hand in dealing with employees. (6) Female Episcopalians formed national organizations in order to gain a strong voice in the national church: the Woman's Auxiliary to the Board of Missions (1871), the triennial of the Women of the Church (1874), and the United Thank Offering (1889). (7) Episcopalians expanded their ministry to blacks (Bishop Payne Divinity School in Petersburg, Virginia, began to prepare black clergy in 1878), orientals (Deaconess Drant's True Sunshine Mission to Chinese-Americans in San Francisco opened in 1905), hispanics and other groups. (8) The Reverend Thomas Gallaudet (1822-1902) led the way in opening the church to the deaf.[6]

This unit will help participants understand the creation of the modern Episcopal Church with a national as well as diocesan structure. It will also show that social concerns have been an integral part of the Episcopal Church's mission for many years. The role of women in the church is just now beginning to be affirmed. Historical studies are showing the significance of movements toward ordination of women, beginning with deaconesses, as well as the inclusion of lay women at all levels of lay leadership and authority in the church. Unfortunately, as has been noted, it seems that men did most of the writing about their faith while women acted on theirs. We hope that future revisions of this book will include more significant documents from the past by women as they become available.

What Is Needed for This Session

Copies of *The Book of Common Prayer*.

Beginning the Session

Open with the Litany of Thanksgiving, No. 2, *The Book of Common Prayer*, pages 836-837.

After the prayer, ask whether there are any questions. You may want to list these on newsprint or a blackboard. If some will be covered in the activities, say so now. Short, factual questions can simply be answered by the leader or others in the class and need not be listed.

First Activity

Present a mini-lecture based (given either by you, as leader, or by a designated person) on the ecumenical documents in these readings. Follow this with a 15 minute round-table discussion.

OR

Spend no more than five minutes developing a brief definition of ecumenism, just to be sure that everyone is talking about the same thing. Then, divide participants into two groups. Have one group make a list of as many reasons as possible for ecumenism. The other group will list arguments against. Allow 10 minutes for preparation; then spend 10 minutes on the reports.

Second Activity

Ask each member to complete, in writing, the following:

"In the early part of this century, some Episcopal clergy and lay were actively involved in socialism. I (agree or do not agree) that they should have done this because. . ."

Allow no more than 5 minutes for this activity.

After 5 minutes, invite people to read their answers. There should be no comments allowed by anyone other than the person reading. After all who wish to respond have done so, lead a general discussion on this subject.

If You Have an Hour and a Half—Add This Activity

Present a mini-lecture (given either by you, as leader, or a person designated) on the role of women in the church.

OR

Divide participants into two groups. Ask each group to list the changes in women's involvement in the church that were revealed in this and Unit 5. Allow 10 minutes for this activity and another 15 minutes for reporting. Pay careful attention to the similarities in the two lists. After the reporting, read the quotation from Vida Scudder in the Resource Book (Reading 5). Discuss Scudder's comment.

If You Have Two Hours—Add This Activity

Turn to the questions in "Pulling Everything Together" in the Resource Book. Discuss as many of them as possible with the full group.

Closing Activity

You will need to adjust the time spent on the preceding activities to allow at least 2 minutes for each member of your group in the final activity. Because this is the last session, ask each to state, briefly, the most important thing learned in the course.

Close the course with the appropriate form of Daily Devotions in *The Book of Common Prayer*, pages 136-140.

Special Note: For One or More Sessions After The Course Is Completed—

For a particularly active group, you might find it worthwhile to schedule one or more additional meetings to discuss current events in the church in light of what was learned in the course. If you do this, it will be a good idea to set the agenda before the session (for example, to discuss women's ordination) rather than let the session be a free-for-all. The agenda, of course, should be set in consultation with those who will participate. It will also be wise to limit participants to those who have completed *Making Sense of the Episcopal Church*. It may also be a good idea to take a break of at least three weeks before scheduling further sessions.

Notes

1. Holmes, Urban T. III. *What is Anglicanism?* Harrisburg, PA: Morehouse Publishing, 1982, vii-viii.

2. Woolverton, John F. *Colonial Anglicanism In North America.* Detroit: Wayne State University Press, 1984, 15.

3. Manross, W.W. *A History of the American Episcopal Church.* New York: Morehouse-Gorham Company, 1959, 172.

4. Prichard, Robert W. *A History of the Episcopal Church.* Harrisburg, PA: Morehouse Publishing, 1991, 105-106.

5. *Ibid.*, 137-138.

6. Prichard, Robert W., ed. *Readings From The History of The Episcopal Church.* Wilton, CT: Morehouse-Barlow, 1986, 115.